Würzburg
Scenes of a City

20.08.2005

Happy Birthday Linda

Best Regards

Sven and Family

from Würzburg, Germany

Sven Schmidt
Kister Str. 34
D - 97204 Höchberg
Germany

Johann Bapist Homann: A bird's eye view from the north of Würzburg as a fortified Baroque town; colored copperplate engraving based on Balthasar Neumann's 1723 layout including the Residenz.

Imprint:

3. revised edition 2001
© Elmar Hahn Verlag, Veitshöchheim

Idea and concept: Elmar Hahn, Klaus Schinagl
Photography: Elmar Hahn, Veitshöchheim
Text: Dr. Peter Schreiber, Würzburg
Interpretation in English: Tina Neil, Würzburg
Layout: Klaus Schinagl, Veitshöchheim
Litho: digiline GmbH Medienservice, Veitshöchheim
Production: Karo-Druck OHG, Frangart

Printed in Europe

ISBN 3-98O2214-4-X

Würzburg

Scenes of a City

Photography: Elmar Hahn
Text: Peter Schreiber
Design: Klaus Schinagl

elmar
hahn
verlag

Lovely, Magnificent City

The choice of these two particular adjectives is not accidental and although they often tend to be overused, they were the words Wolfgang Amadeus Mozart chose to describe this city a year before his death. Mozart was in Würzburg during a brief stopover in which he fortified his "dear stomach" with a cup of coffee on his way from Vienna to Frankfurt where he was to be a part of the imperial coronation. Although his stay was no longer than the time needed to change horses, he intuitively managed to capture the atmosphere of the "Herbipolis" and wrote his impressions to his wife Constanze in 1790.

"Herbipolis" means "City of Herbs" and was derived from the supposition that "Würz" (German: herbs) must have had something to do with herbs or seasonings. Thus the origin of the Latin-Greek hybrid out of herba and polis (city-state). Sebastian Münster mentioned "Wirtzburg" in his famous cosmography in 1548. Nineteen years later he wrote that "ordinary people are involved in growing wine, something that grows in excess".

Throughout the years it was only natural that poets, scholars and artists should pay homage to the city and describe it in a variety of ways. As early as the 12th century Gottfried von Viterbo saw it "as a paradise on Earth". Konrad von Würzburg wrote in the 13th century: "architectural genius had a hand in the building of the city which abounds in wealth and prestige". Heinrich von Kleist, Johann Wolfgang von Goethe, Richard Wagner, Felix Dahn, Wilhelm von Scholz, Rudolf G. Binding and Gertrud von le Fort – just to name a few – each had a special relationship to Würzburg and each expressed his or her feelings in a most personal manner. In 1912 the lyric poet from

Würzburg, Max Dauthendey, wrote: "I was just a young man when Professor Röntgen discovered the X-ray here in the physics laboratory creating a new light that penetrates the human body and makes it visible to the naked eye. Later, I often said to myself that the X-ray could only have been discovered in Würzburg because it is only here that a secret light comes so close to mankind". Hermann Hesse confessed in 1930: "If I were a future writer trying to decide where my birthplace should be, I would seriously take Würzburg into consideration".

It is not purely coincidental that time and again the characteristics that make Würzburg what it is have been reason enough to inspire artists and scientists alike. Neither should the impression be given that the city is without flaw. Yet its location, its cheerful charm with its Mediterranean ambience nestled in the Main River valley and sur-

rounded by vineyards, emits a special feeling somewhat uncommon to city life – a feeling that doesn't first arise upon seeing the majestic fortress and the silhouette of its towers.

The enthusiastic visitor will soon discover the unmistakable. This book is intended as a guide to help make the unmistakable more readily apparent.

A stroll through Würzburg will not only reveal the contrasts between old and new; the discrepancies between the past and the present will be made evident in the liveliness and the hustle and bustle of the city as well. No matter where one walks, however, one will have to admit that W.A. Mozart was perfectly correct in calling Würzburg a "lovely, magnificent city".

Historical Dates

Circa 1000 B.C. a Celtic fortress is set up on the hill on the left side of the Main River

Circa 500 B.C. the prince's residence is established on the hill with a fishing village below

Circa 100 B.C. German tribes take over the country

Circa 450 B.C. Würzburg is mentioned as "Urburzis" – an Alemannian city

Circa 650 A.D. the first seat of the Frankish dukedom can be found on the right banks of the Main

689 the martyrdom of the Irish missionaries Kilian, Kolonat and Totnam marks the beginning of Christianity in Franconia

704 first official record of "Castellum Virteburch"

706 the consecration of the first church on the "Würzburg", today the Marienberg

742 St. Bonifatius founds the bishopric; Burkard is the first bishop

752 discovery of Kilian's grave – today the site of the Neumünster Church

788 consecration of the first Cathedral in the presence of Charlemagne

1030 the right to coin money, collect toll and the right to hold market is granted; the city of kings becomes the city of bishops

1133 the first stone bridge across the Main is erected

1156 Emperor Frederick Barbarossa takes the marriage vows with his second wife, Beatrice of Burgundy and in

1168 Frederick Barbarossa confers the ducal title on the bishop of Würzburg during the Reichstag in Würzburg

1201 the fortress in founded on the Marienberg; Würzburg has approximately 5000 inhabitants; circa

1230 Walther von der Vogelweide is buried in the Lusam Garden of the Neumünster Collegiate Church

1253 Bishop Lobdeburg moves his residence from the town to the fortress

1256 the first elected town council and mayor

1262 Albertus Magnus sojourns in Würzburg

1287 the German National Council convenes in the Cathedral

1316 the city buys the "Grafeneckart" building to be used as a town hall

1319 wealthy citizens found the hospital "Zum Heiligen Geist"

1348 pogrom on what is now the Market Place

1397 King Wenceslaus the Lazy promises to make Würzburg a free imperial city but soon reneges on his pledge

1402-1413 the founding of the first university in Würzburg

1483 Tilman Riemenschneider arrives in Würzburg

1518 Martin Luther in Würzburg

1531 death of Tilman Riemenschneider

1576 Prince-Bishop Julius Echter von Mespelbrunn establishes the hospital Juliusspital and in

1582 the Julius University

1631-1634 the Swedes under King Gustav Adolf lay siege to the town and the Marienberg

1711 Balthasar Neumann arrives in Würzburg; as of

1719 the prince-bishops again reside in the town

1720 cornerstone of the Residenz is laid

1745 Empress Maria Theresia in Würzburg

1753 death of Balthasar Neumann

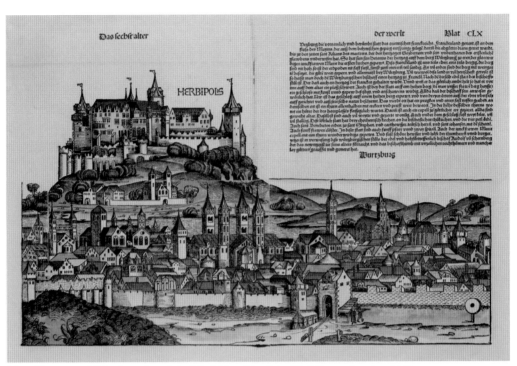

The oldest view of Würzburg from Schedel's "Chronicle of the World"; woodcarving 1493.

1796 Archduke Charles of Austria defeats the troops of the French Revolution under Jourdan in the battle by Würzburg

1802 the prince-bishopric is secularized; Würzburg is annexed to Bavaria

1805 the city and principality of Franconia are turned over to Ferdinand of Toscany

1814 final integration into Bavaria

1815-1825 King Ludwig I resides as crown prince in Würzburg; circa

1830 Würzburg has 22,000 inhabitants

1833 Richard Wagner sojourns as choir director at the Würzburg Theater; he composes his first opera "The Fairies"

1841 the beginning of large-scale commercial shipping on the Main

1854 Würzburg is linked to the German railroad network

1860 Würzburg has 33,000 inhabitants

1866 during the Austro-Prussian War the Prussians bombard the fortifications

1867 the city is no longer fortified

1895 Röntgen discovers the X-ray (Nobel Prize in 1901)

1900 Würzburg has 75,000 inhabitants

1922 first Mozart Festival in Würzburg

1934 Würzburg has 100,000 inhabitants

1945 on March 16th the Royal Air Force attacks and destroys 82% of the city in 17 minutes

1965 the enlargement of the university on the outskirts of the city

1995 the Siebold Museum opens its doors

1997 the Würzburg Cultural Foundation is established

1998 the Riemenschneider Hall in the Mainfränkisches Museum is refurbished

2000 the Market Place and the Juliuspromenade are modernized; Würzburg has 126,000 inhabitants

The Fortress on the Hill

High above the Main and St. Burkard's Church lies the fortress Marienberg. Below it, boats rock back and forth in the river that meanders its way through the hills covered with vineyards lined up in accurate formation. The grape vines have taken over the Schlossberg and soak in the warm rays of the midday sun that shines brightly onto the slopes between the fortress and the 1200 year old church.

Here, high above a propitious ford in the river is where the history of Würzburg began. Fragments of broken pottery and archeological finds over a thousand years old suggest the possibility of a ring wall. The German tribes came, then the Franks and finally, the Irish-Scotish wandering monks Kilian, Kolonat and Totnam whose martyr-

Fortress Marienberg.
Previous pages: Kiliansturm (Kilian's Tower).
Left: Marienberg from the northeast.
Below: Nocturnal view from the south of the fortress with the Machicolation Tower dominating in the foreground.

dom enabled Christianity to take root. The oldest building on the hill was erected and consecrated in honor of the Virgin Mary: the round Mary's Church constructed at the beginning of the 7th century. The eye takes in the castle keep and the well house that was walled up from the time of the Swedish invasion until the 1930's and then it wanders from one fortress corner tower to the next – an ensemble that makes for an impressive sight.

It was Konrad von Querfurt who first began to fortify the Marienberg at the beginning of the 13th century. The round tower in the middle of the inner courtyard dates back to this period as well as the predecessor of the present day Kilian Tower that is now crowned by a modern golden statue of St. Kilian. Moreover, there is the lovely Renaissance temple that houses the deep well that has its source at the Main over 100 meters below.

Already in the Middle Ages the "Fortress of the Holy Virgin Mary" served the bishops

as a temporary residence and it was these very bishops that continued to see to the further construction and expansion of the fortifications. In 1495, Rudolf II von Scherenberg, already in the tenth decade of his life and a man who could look back on almost 30 years in office, had the fortifications modernized, the Main Gate renovated and the ring wall that had been constructed under his predecessor, Otto von Wolfskeel, improved. As early as 1493 the Nuremberg doctor and humanist, Hartmut Schedel, described the fortress in his famous Chronicle of the World.

The peasants' attempts to attack these fortifications and thus establish authority were futile. It was the prince-bishop's troops that were victorious in Würzburg during the Peasants' War. It was Tilman Riemenschneider, the famous stone sculptor, woodcarver and for a short time mayor of the town, who, having rather accidentally sided with the rebellious peasants, was thrown into the Randersacker Tower and tortured.

The fortress today looks much like it did between 1573 and 1617 during the days of Julius Echter von Mespelbrunn, the Prince-Bishop and Counter-Reformer, who implemented the Renaissance style, sometimes known as the Echter style in this region.

What the peasants were unable to accomplish was readily accomplished by the army of Gustav Adolf of Sweden. Luck was on their side as they laid siege to the fortress and flushed with victory, they plundered virtually every nook and cranny of the castle including the sumptuous leather-bound library of the prince-bishop. The library made its way to Uppsala where it can still be admired. Even today in the shade of the Randersacker Tower, one can't fail to notice a delightful bay gallery from the Echter era that connects the former library to the so-called emporer's chambers. Opposite, on the northern court front in the shade of the Marienturm (Mary's Tower) is the Bibra spiral staircase that was built in 1511 and named after the Prince-Bishop Lorenz von Bibra. This staircase winds around a hollow newel with

A rather unusual view of the Marienberg and its towers.

13

three columns inside and used to give access to the various floors.

The "princely" garden at the front of the castle was laid out during the Baroque and Rococo periods. By 1712 a new arsenal and commandant's building designed by Balthasar Neumann's mentor and teacher, Andreas Müller, had been erected. Today, one corner of the former headquarters serves as the entrance to the Mainfränkisches Museum. The facades of the buildings were restored in 1989.

In 1719 the prince-bishop moved from the fortress atop the Marienberg back into the town, at first taking up residence in the Rosenbach Palace. It would take over a decade before the prince-bishops could rule from the more spacious quarters of the Residenz which would continue to be under construction for years to come.

The fortress became a barracks and an arsenal. The year 1724 saw the beginning of construction on the Machicolation Tower halfway up the southwest slope known as the Leistengrund. The tower gets its name from the openings in the floor of the parapet through which hot liquids and heavy stones could be dropped.

The disorders of the French Revolution were followed by the dissolving of the bishopric through secularization in 1803. The military importance of the fortifications continued to decline until in 1867 the town ceased to be a fortress altogether. In 1870-71, however, 1800 French prisoners of war were still being housed in a section of the fortress.

After World War II the fortifications were in extremely poor condition and could only be used as emergency housing. The extensive renovations that had taken place in the 1930's were annihilated in the course of a single night in March 1945 when the Royal Air Force conducted an air attack on Würzburg. Reconstruction has largely been carried out to completion. It took over 40 million marks to stabilize the bastions alone.

Fortress Marienberg: Left: Gothic Scherenberg Gate. Below: Interior of Mary's Church.
Following pages: Marienkirche (Mary's Church) – and Randersacker Tower.

A Master Craftsman and Much More

The Mainfränkisches Museum located within the walls of the fortress is one of the most impressive of its kind. Not only is it known for its regional treasures that span the centuries, the museum is also just as renowned for its supraregional collections and special exhibits. This internationally famous museum attracts art lovers worldwide.

There were plans to erect a municipal museum as early as 1889. In 1913 the Franconian Luitpold Museum opened its doors and in 1938-39 the rooms in the Fürstenbau that displayed the history of the city and the fortress were completed. In 1945 the museum lay in all but total ruin and more than half of its treasures were lost forever. Fortunately, some of the museum's treasures could be brought to safety in time but many of the artifacts lay buried in the

rubble and ruin. It was a bold undertaking to re-establish the museum in the arsenal and the Echter Bastion of the Marienberg.

Today, the late Gothic works of Master Til in the Riemenschneider Hall are one of the main attractions of the museum which has over a quarter of a million visitors a year. Riemenschneider's "Maria von Acholshausen" is one of the most brilliant examples of grief and suffering that has ever been expressed in wood. In 1981 over 200,000

Left: Mary in Mourning by Tilman Riemenschneider around 1515. Below: Riemenschneider's effigy in the Cathedral cemetery.

Riemenschneider's Adam and Eve (1492/93) are on display in the Mainfränkisches Museum. Copies of these sandstone figures are located on the south portal of Mary's Chapel.

Late Bronze Age (1000 B.C.) ritual wagon (miniature) from a chambered tomb near Acholshausen.

people visited a special Riemenschneider exhibit which displayed the early works of the Würzburg master including loans from such diverse places as Amsterdam, Vienna, Graz, Berlin, Munich, Cologne, Cleveland and New York City.

Riemenschneider was born in Heiligenstadt in 1460, the son of a minter and coppersmith, he came to his uncle's in Würzburg where he settled down having completed his apprenticeship and travels. A very productive master in his trade, he was respected and then ostracized – he died a broken man in 1531 having outlived three of his four wives. He was totally forgotten until the discovery of his effigy in the Cathedral cemetery in 1822.

The red sandstone effigy (page 18) depicts a man dressed in the style typical of a 16th century burgher wearing a toque. His folded hands are holding a rosary and between his legs is Riemenschneider's blazon with cut and crossed straps to signify his name ("Riemen" means straps in German; "schneiden" means to cut). The inscription reads:

"Anno dm (domini) MCCCCCXXXI (1531) on the eve of kiliani (July 7th) died the honourable and artistic Tilman Riemenschneider, sculptor, burgher of Würzburg. God be merciful to him. Amen." Riemenschneider's son, Jörg, designed the effigy in memory of his father. Ten years later, a second inscription in memory of Riemenschneider's son-in-law, Bernhard Hop, was added. A copy of this effigy stands on the northern outside wall of the Cathedral. But now back to the museum!

Whether it be headman's swords and weapons, religious paintings in the Church Hall historical paintings and portraits in the Stone Hall or the masterpieces of Tiepolo and Zick in the gallery – whether it be the Bozetti Collection (small sculptures from the estate of the court sculptor Johann Peter Wagner) or the mercy seat of God to be found among the Gothic sculpture: the vastness and diversity of treasures offer something of interest for everyone. The historical rooms in all their richness display: faience in the Crafts Hall, garden statues by Ferdinand Tietz; a music stand and grandfather's clock in the Rococo Room; an ostentatious writing table in the Tapestry Hall; an old clock and Riemenschneider's graceful female figures in the Gothic Room; a magnificent alabaster gravestone and linden wood relief from the school of Veit Stoß in the Knight's Hall; Riemenschneider's splendid late Gothic table in the Bastion Corridor; religious and secular artifacts of silver and gold, silk embroidery and religious relics in the Kilian Hall; folklore; prehistoric artifacts, Romanesque sculpture; Franconian viticulture in the Wine-Press Hall; and the Casemate.

The "Friends of Main-Franconian History and Art" have been holding concerts for the past 25 years in the Schönborn Hall whose walls are abundant with priceless effigies.

In 1990 the Fürstenbau Museum opened in the south wing of the fortifications. The first

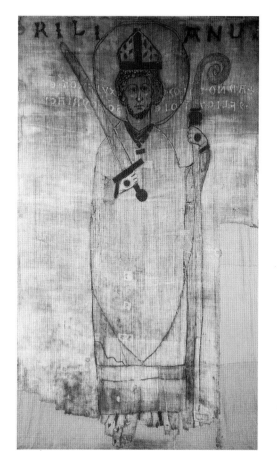

Above: This old clock still with the original clockwork dates back to around 1350 and could have been used by a tower watchman.
Left: Kilian's Banner from 1266 is the oldest war flag in Germany.

floor contains reconstructions of the former prince-bishops' apartments as they may have looked before the prince-bishops moved to the Residenz. The furnishings, however, are from the 17th century. A thorn reliquary and other valuable works of art from the Court Church are on display in a treasure chamber along with a display of lovely vestments and sacred vessels.

The second floor of this museum displays the history of the city of Würzburg from the arrival of Kilian in the 7th century to the present day. Of special interest is the Kilian Banner (1266) which is said to be the oldest German banner in existence. A sample of silk embroidery from the year 980 as well as models of Würzburg as the town appeared in 1525 and in 1945 after its destruction are among the other objects of interest.

The fortress Marienberg which is owned and under the charge of the Free State of Bavaria not only houses the Mainfränkisches Museum and its administrative offices but a portion of the state archives. Furthermore, the city's tourist bureau has convention rooms and a banquet hall as well as a restaurant and the pub "To the Old Watch" within its walls.

A walk around the fortress offers many splendid views of the city and its numerous towers, the Main River flowing peacefully below and on the next hill, Balthasar Neumann's Pilgrimage Church, the "Käppele" with its graceful 35 meter high spires. Vineyards seem to cover every inch of the slopes. The "Stein" vineyards come into view upon crossing the dry moat to the Scherenberg Gate. Connoisseurs of the superb Franconian wines nod knowingly upon hearing the locations "Stein" and "Leiste".

The fortress Marienberg at sunset.
Following pages: The Old Main Bridge with its 12 larger than life sandstone figures spans the 125 meter river below the Marienberg.

Enzelin's Risk

Presumably some sort of link between the banks of the Main existed as early as the middle of the 8th century at the time of Bishop Burkhard. Yet it wasn't until 1133 that Master Enzelin built the first sturdy bridge. Enzelin was a gifted layman whose plans for the unusually wide spans of the bridge meant that a certain amount of risk was involved. The bridge, however, held 209 years before a flood carried it away. The bridge that replaced it suffered from the same fate 100 years later. Next, a wooden bridge was constructed as an interim solution until Master Hans von Königshofen could begin work on a strong bridge out of stone and wood in 1474. The financing of this bridge was not always an easy matter; the bridge was paid for by indulgences and due to a lack of money, the wooden piers were not arched until 1536. Court sessions were held on the bridge on the first Wednesday of every month in good weather until 1554. Over the years, the wooden piers were replaced with stone and the gates and towers were torn down as they no longer appealed to the tastes of the times. In times of war the bridge was always under heavy attack: in 1631, 1813 and 1866. It was heavily bombed in the Second World War and renovation was not completed until 1977.

Approaching the city from the west, the 125 meter long Old Bridge offers an impressive panorama of the heart of the city: the statues on the bays of the piers, the Town Hall and the spires of the Cathedral unite in perfect harmony. This view can only begin to be matched by the Charles Bridge in Prague. Twelve stone Baroque statues, copies of the originals, flank the bridge. These are saints, for the most part, whose lives were closely linked with the history of Würzburg or the lives of their donors: Kilian, Kolonat, Totnam, the Virgin as the patron saint Franconia, Burkard, Bruno, Charlemagne, C. Borromäus, Nepomuk, Joseph, Fridericus and Pippin.

Old Main Bridge with a view of the Grafeneckart and the Cathedral.

The Death of a Viscount

A nobleman just below a count is a viscount or deputy to a count. During the Middle Ages, however, the term was also used to mean count (in German: Graf). A certain Mr. Eckart, who as of 1193 had the honor of being a mayor and a burggrave all in one, lived in a medieval family tower that in 1212 had been given the name "Curia Eggehardi Comitis" – or administrative office of Eckart the Count.

Background information aside. A good view of the "Grafeneckart", the oldest portion of the Town Hall, can be enjoyed from the "Vierröhren" Fountain directly across the street. To the west of the "Grafeneckart" is the "Red Building" dating back to 1659/60 and to its left, a new addition which was

constructed on the site of the former Carmelite Monastery after its destruction during World War II.

Unfortunately, the viscount, after whom the building was named, was murdered on the 13th of December in 1201 by the two brothers Bodo von Ravensburg and Heinrich Hund von Falkenberg, who less than a year

Grafeneckart (Town Hall) and Baroque Fountain (Vierröhrenbrunnen). Left: The 13th century Wenzel Hall in the Town Hall.

later also murdered his benefactor, Bishop Konrad von Querfurt. It remains unclear whether or not this act of revenge was ever atoned for.

The south facade of this building is also known as the "Green Tree" after the fresco painting. During the Peasants' War, this served as the site where the prince-bishop took his enemies prisoner, among them, Tilman Riemenschneider.

It was in the Wenceslaus Hall that King Wenceslaus was wined and dined by the city fathers, but to practically no avail. The King promised to make Würzburg a free imperial city but he reneged on his pledge almost immediately after his departure.

Across from the "Grafeneckart" the four cardinal virtues adorn the Baroque Fountain that is crowned by the patron saint Franconia (1766).

A Whooping Crane at the Banks of the River

The first crane on the banks of the Main dates back to 1560. The word is derived from the whooping crane whose long neck can often be seen stretching out into the water. Würzburg's "Old Crane" is one of its more prominent landmarks.

The present crane was built by the son of Balthasar Neumann, Franz Ignaz Michael. After six years of construction, the crane began operation in 1773. The Second World War left the crane untouched and thus intact. Renovations in 1837, 1954 and 1967 were necessary to keep the crane in good working order.

The wooden gears of its two revolving arms can lift up to 4000 pounds. A double treading wheel is the source of power. An iron crane was erected downstream in 1846 and in 1875 work began on the Old Harbor northwest of the municipal heating plant.

In 1922 the iron crane was torn down and the Old Crane, having served its purpose, was shut down. Work on the New Harbor started in 1934. Based on total turnover, Würzburg's three harbors today rank second in Bavaria. They serve as a point of unloading for oil, fodder, construction materials and grain.

To the east of the Old Crane where seagulls love to linger now stands the newly-constructed "House of Franconian Wines" on the site of the former Customs House. Here, the wide selection of fine wines that Franconia is famous for can be tasted and enjoyed in a unique atmosphere.

Previous pages and below: The Old Crane on the banks of the Main River.
Right: The city that is crowned with towers: The Cathedral, the Neumünster Church and Mary's Chapel.

A Dedication in Stone

The story behind Mary's Chapel (Marienka-pelle) at the Market Place is closely inter-twined with the history of the city. Unlike the round Mary's Church (Marienkirche) within the walls of the fortifications, this church, although larger in size, is called a chapel, probably due to the fact that it does not enjoy the rights of a parish church. The Market Place was first laid out at the end of the 14th century and covered the approximate area of the former Jewish ghetto. On an April night in 1349 the area went up in flames. In repentance, the town's inhabitants erected a small chapel, most probably out of wood, on the site of the former synagogue. In 1377 the foundation stone for the "Chapel of the Most Holy Virgin at the Jewish Square in the City of Würtzburg" was laid. Mary's Chapel, which truly represents a culmination of Gothic architecture in Würzburg, is not only a symbol of self-confident burghers but a dedication in stone to the Virgin Mary as well.

The nave and its side aisles of equal height blend in perfectly with the High Gothic choir. The Neo-Gothic spire with its Baroque Virgin is 72 meters high.

Of great interest are the church's three portals. The tympanum of the south portal opening onto the lower Market Square depicts the Coronation of the Virgin. The columns adorning the portal bear copies of Tilman Riemenschneider's famous Adam and Eve. The originals (1493) of these early masterpieces of Würzburg's renowned sculptor and woodcarver can be seen in the Mainfränkisches Museum. Master Til was contracted by the city council to sculpture the stone figures and Riemenschneider created the pair in the nude – something that had not previously been the practice. Adam, 189 cm high, exactly three fingers taller than the master sculptor himself, is depicted without the typical attribute of masculinity – he is beardless.

Left: Mary's Chapel by night.
Right: Effigy for Konrad von Schaumberg in Mary's Chapel (Riemenschneider, 1502).

The tympanum of the west portal represents the Last Judgment. The tympanum above the north portal (beginning of the 15th century) is a unique representation of the Annunciation and Incarnation: God the Father allows the Christ Child to slide down a tube, the Holy Ghost, to the Virgin's left ear.

Christus Salvator created the stone copies of John the Baptist and the 12 Apostles that decorate the niches of the columns. The originals (after 1500) by Riemenschneider and his workshop can also be found in the Mainfränkisches Museum.

The interior of the church, where the members of several noble families are buried, is characterized by its pure Gothic style and by the way light fills the room. Among the numerous effigies that adorn the walls, Riemenschneider's effigy for Bishop von Scherenberg and Bishop von Bibra's war minister, Konrad von Schaumberg, deserve special notice. Konrad died on his way home from the Holy Land and the town council fulfilled the knight's last wishes to have his faithful horse led thrice around the altar and to commission Balthasar Neumann to design his memorial. Neumann is buried within the walls of the church as well.

Andreas Gärtner's Napoleanic obelisque fountain (1805) dominates the lower Market Place. In front of the lovely Renaissance building, the Casteller Hof, stands a bronze statue of a postrider (1974) by Otto Sonnleitner. The market woman (1973) at the upper end of the lower Market Place is also a piece of Sonnleitner's work. House number 14/16 was first built by Balthasar Neumann.

The Gothic nave of Mary's Chapel at the Market Place.

The House to the Falcon on the upper Market Place.

A Falcon on the Roof

The falcon perched atop the central gable of the "House to the Falcon" has always made the building easy to locate. From 1338 to 1406 it was the home of the Cathedral's priest. The foundations of the current building date back to the 17th century.

From 1629 on, the building served as an inn and the innkeeper's widow, Frau Meissner, hired a group of Upper Bavarian craftsmen to redo the facade with a delicate layer of stucco in the patrician Rococo style. This was the perfect counterbalance to the princely Rococo of the Residenz. After all, an innkeeper needed to advertise and because her building already had a special name, she had the falcon set on the rooftop as the final confirmation. It is a fact that the building has had more owners than any other in Würzburg with the exception of the Cathedral chapter houses. The facade was renovated in 1924 and again after its destruction during the Second World War. It soon became the city's jewel of ornamentation and Frau Meissner received her due reward – she was charged no property taxes for a ten year period. The Coronation of the Virgin further enhances the facade.

The city has owned the edifice only since 1939 and it now houses Würzburg's cultural affairs office including the Mozart Festival Office as well as the public library with its new addition to the rear.

Following pages: The upper Market Place with Mary's Chapel and the House to the Falcon as a backdrop bustles with life.

The Founder's Work

"Fiery flames brought down the work of the founder but his spirit was our command. With the help and the power of the Almighty, this new building could be erected. A.D. 1952"

These words are written above the entrance portal of the Juliusspital. Whoever enters the hospital complex from the Juliuspromenade is taken aback at first by the beauty and harmony of the buildings and gardens. In 1576, on the grounds that had been used as a Jewish cemetery since the 12th century, the founder Prince-Bishop Julius Echter von Mespelbrunn had the cornerstone laid for "the poor, weary and poverty-stricken as well as for the sick, the weak and the abandoned". The architect was probably Georg Robijn from Mainz. Gustav Adolf of Sweden left the hospital funds undisturbed because the foundation's epistle warned that anyone who attempted to lay hands on foundation property would be damned on Judgment Day. The King of Sweden: "I don't want to have anything

to do with these priests in the next world."

The charitable institution was visited by fire several times in the course of the centuries and renowned architects such as Petrini, Neumann, Greising, Geigel and Gärtner contributed immensely towards the complex's appearance and repeated reconstructions. The hospital complex whose founder had richly endowed it with vineyards was nothing but rubble in 1945.

It was closely connected with the university until 1854. Famous doctors and professors such as Siebold, Koelliker and Virchow held lectures in the auditorium of the garden pavilion which at the time was known as the "Anatomical Theater". Nowadays this festive auditorium is used for concerts and representative purposes.

One should not hesitate to catch a glimpse of the garden's resplendent Baroque fountain located behind the castle-like complex. It was created by Jacob van der Auwera in 1706. An eagle, the heraldic symbol of the

Rococo pharmacy in the Juliusspital.

Baroque fountain by Jacob van der Auwera.

Prince-Bishop Johann Philipp von Greiffen-clau, is surrounded by dolphins and four figures symbolizing the four rivers of the bishopric in Würzburg: the Main, the Saale, the Sinn and the Tauber.

Among the prestigious doctors who worked in the Juliusspital were the Siebolds. The doctor and Japanese scholar, Philipp Franz von Siebold (1796–1866), who is highly-esteemed in Japan, is also highly-respected in his own country.

The combination of a hospital, an old age home and a winery has always ensured success. The winery, like its other two sisters in Würzburg – the Bürgerspital zum Heili-gen Geist and the state-run Hofkeller – own some of the sunniest vineyards in all Franconia. Who, then, can be surprised that an institution that can store around 720,000 litres of wine in wooden vats, 600,000 litres in stainless steel tanks and 400,000 in bottles also has its own bakery and a charming wine inn at its disposal. Wine can be purchased on the premises. In an arcaded passageway hangs a sign that reminds one of the past: "Infusions dispensed in the Wine-Pressing Hall"!

Following pages: The towers and steeples of the Cathedral, the Neumünster and St. John's and the Town Hall.

St. Kilian's Sepulchre and Walther's Grave

Cater-corner from the Market Place the eleventh century Romanesque basilica, the Neumünster Church, stands on the site of Würzburg's first Cathedral. Its magnificent red sandstone facade was added between 1710 and 1716 by Johann Dientzenhofern and Joseph Greising. The sculpture work was carried out by Johann van der Auwera: the basilica's saints John the Baptist and the Evangelist John adorn the Main Portal; in the gable above is the Ascension of Mary followed by Christus Salvator holding the orb of sovereignty and flanked by St. Kilian and St. Burkard (inside) and Kolonat (holding the Grail) and Totnam (holding the Gospels). The shield of the Prince-Bishop J. Ph. von Greiffenclau decorates the triangular gable. The majestic octagonal dome and the Late Romanesque octagonal bell tower with its Baroque onion roof loom from behind the stunning facade. The church's interior is also noteworthy: the High Altar (1724), the decorative paintings of the nave, transept and crossing and the dome fresco.

Other treasures include an early Gothic crucifix with Christ's arms laid across his chest (before 1350) and a sandstone madonna (1493) by Tilman Riemenschneider.

St. Kilian's sepulchre (Kiliansgruft) designates the spot where Kilian, Kolonat and Totnam were martyred in 689. From of old, the altar with its reliquary and Franconian apostels has been a place of pilgrimage.

The 13th century minnesinger, Walther von der Vogelweide, lies buried in the Lusam Garden (Lusamgärtlein). Frederick II bestowed upon him an ecclesiastical benefice which allowed him to spend his later days at the Neumünster Church. The name "Lusam" is derived from the monks' Latin "Lusus" meaning "game" or "recreation" and thus a "leisure time" garden. One side of the small garden is bordered by the remaining arcade side of the Neumünster cloisters dating back to the Hohenstaufen (1170/80).

Left: The Baroque facade of the Neumünster Church.
Below: Cloisters gallery in the Lusam Garden with a Romanesque relief of Christ.

Soon to Turn 1000

The Cathedral in Würzburg has not always been St. Kilian's Cathedral. The first Cathedral, which was consecrated to Christus Salvator in the presence of Charlemagne in 788 by Bishop Berowelf, was located on the site of the present day Neumünster Church. This Cathedral was destroyed by fire in 855. A smaller church then had to make room for Bishop Arno's Carolingian edifice which was followed by the first St. Kilian's, a somewhat smaller version of the Cathedral today. Bishops Thioto and Heinrich I expanded the Cathedral after another fire had again done its damage. Around the year 1000 St. Andreas was made the patron of the Cathedral and remained so until 1967.

Bishop Bruno, a Salian, was the actual founder of the Cathedral as it stands today, the fourth largest Romanesque church in Germany after the imperial cathedrals at Speyer, Mainz and Worms. Around 1040 Benno began with his renovation plans for an overall rebuilding of the church and upon his death, the crypt was dedicated in his name (1045). Benno's plans could not be fully carried out until 1188 and in 1287 the sole German National Council convened in this church.

The Cathedral has had many faces over the centuries: Julius Echter's plans († 1617) were being carried out until the 18th century. Between 1701 and 1704 Pietro Magno had the entire interior redone with a fine layer of stucco in the High Baroque style. From 1721 to 1736 Balthasar Neumann added the Schönborn Chapel onto the north transept. Under Neumann, various other building changes within the Cathedral itself were undertaken, all of which were transformed into Neo-Romanesque and Neo-Gothic after the secularization. The Cathedral was virtually destroyed in 1945 and many of the church's treasures, among them works by T. Riemenschneider, were lost forever. In 1946 more damage occurred when new timber rafters collapsed taking a portion of the walls with it. Reconstruction was finally completed in 1967.

East side of the Cathedral.

47

The outer appearance is both powerful and fortresslike, even plain if not monotonous. Although the beauty of the exterior as well as the interior of the church is disputable, there can be no debate as to the Cathedral's sacred and historical significance or its function as the center of religion. The west end with its 73 meter high towers that somehow seem to stand unusually close to each other has been adapted to the old silhouette. On the east end, the two slender spires that become octagonal above the church roof are certainly more appealing. They date back to 1237. The semi-circular apse of the choir is flanked by two low sacristies and thus appears spatially divided and more pleasing than the west end.

A copy of Riemenschneider's effigy hangs on the north wall of the church – the original was discovered in 1822 in the Cathedral cemetery. Its discovery renewed interest in the life and works of the Gothic master sculptor and woodcarver who had somehow been completely forgotten.

The restoration of the interior, which was completed in 1989, is an attempt to recreate that which was destroyed in the past and to get by with as little new creation as possible. The High Altar was moved to the crossing and the choir with the episcopal chair was set up in the apse as a presbytery. The High Altar, the pyx and the bishop's chair were designed by Albert Schilling from Basel and the tabernacle by Josef Amberg from Würzburg. Undoubtedly the Cathedral's most magnificent treasures are the numerous bishops' effigies that have been preserved from as far back as the 12th century. The two most resplendent ones (Prince-Bishops von Bibra and von Scherenberg) are of red marble imported from Salzburg and the work of Tilman Riemenschneider.

Riemenschneider did not idealize his portrayal of the 95-year old Prince-Bishop Rudolf von Scherenberg; instead Riemenschneider presents him as a man who is

Riemenschneider's effigy for Prince-Bishop Rudolf von Scherenberg in the Cathedral.

The interior of the Cathedral.
Below: This stone cross from the Cathedral crypt is considered to be late Carolingian from circa 850.

weighed down by the burden of his miter and his office, a man whose face reflects the high spiritual refinement of a life dedicated to the Church.

In addition to these effigies, there are numerous other noteworthy treasures within the Cathedral: Master Eckart from Worms designed the Baptismal Font (1279) which is the sole surviving larger piece of bronze casting from the 13th century in southern Germany; the stone figure of St. Leonhard (circa 1310); Gothic wall paintings (1380/90); further works by Riemenschneider such as St. John the Evangelist and Christus Salvator; Peter and Andrew on the Apostle Altar as well as the magnificently decorated Pulpit (1609/19) created in the Renaissance style by Michael Kern. The Crypt contains the grave of St. Bruno († 1045) and Balthasar Neumann drew up the plans for the unique Schönborn Chapel. Not to be forgotten is the lovely Organ with its 7000 pipes and "trompets".

Balthasar's Pilgrimage Church

It is no surprise that the "Käppele" (Small Chapel) is one of Würzburg's landmarks – the exquisite religious counterpart to the Marienberg fortress. The lovely setting and the splendid facade attract pilgrims and casual strollers alike.

Around 1640 a fisherman's son took a carved pietà and placed it on a wayside shrine on the Nikolausberg. (Today the pietà is on the altar of the church.) On the 6th of July, 1650, four miracle healings were recorded in connection with the pietà followed by a number of visions and strange occurrences. It was not long before the hill became a regular place of pilgrimage especially during Pentecost when pilgrims sought to have their prayers answered on this sacred spot. Today the path up to the Käppele is lined with huge plane trees that lead past 14 small Rococo chapels in which Christ's path to Calvary is dramatically depicted.

The Small Chapel was widened in 1690 and lengthened in 1713. Finally, Germany's most renowned Baroque architect, Balthasar Neumann, the "artificer of pleasurable and somber buildings", was contracted by the prince-bishop to build a new church. The foundation stone of the church consecrated to the Virgin Mary was laid on the 4th of May, 1748, and work continued on the edifice until 1750. The interior wasn't completed until 1821 and the Käppele was consecrated on September 21, 1824. The church has been renovated and restored several times.

The frescos (1752) were the work of Matthäus Günther and the stucco work was the creation of J.M. Feichtmayr from Wessobrunn. A true demonstration of folk piety can be seen in the Miracle Corridor that is decorated with manifold church votives.

Left: Neumann's Pilgrimage Church "Käppele" (1747/50) on the hill, the Nikolausberg.
Above: Magnificent interior of the Pilgrimage Church.

A Registered Palace

The former Residenz of the prince-bishops in Würzburg including the gardens and forecourt was registered in the World Heritage Listed Sites on January 1, 1982 in accordance with the UNESCO Agreement for the Worldwide Protection of Culture and Natural Heritage. This honour can only underline the significance of this monumental edifice that has been praised far and wide. Napoleon, for example, is said to have called the Residenz the "loveliest parsonage in Europe". Just how did the construction of this "palace of palaces" come about?

In 1253 Bishop Lobdeburg had his administration moved from the Cathedral to the fortress. It is a well-known fact that bishops and burghers did not always see eye to eye, thus the necessity of thick walls between them. It was surely not the easiest of tasks to run the town from the Marienberg and when dangers of life and limb subsided, the prince-bishops contemplated having a residence in the town itself. Johann

Philipp Franz von Schönborn was the first prince-bishop to realize such a plan. It was argued that it would be less expensive to maintain the prince-bishop's household in the town, but, of course, the opposite proved to be true. The Prince-Bishop, as his title indicates, the embodiment of both worldly and spiritual power, managed to obtain 600,000 florins through a lawsuit in the first year of his rule thus ensuring the beginning of construction on this work of architectural genius. Moreover, the name Schönborn was synonymous with a passion for building. We are truly grateful to the Schönborn family although the inhabitants of Würzburg certainly suffered many a hardship during the years of construction (1719-1795).

A total of seven prince-bishops ruled during the completion of the Residenz. Franz von Ingelheim, for example, released Neumann from his contract because the Prince-Bishop preferred spending his time and ef-

The Residenz and its Court Gardens from the south.

forts on alchemy and trying to make gold. His successor's first task was to reinstate Neumann and bestow honour upon honour upon the man who collaborated with the leading architects and artists from Paris, Vienna and Mainz in order to complete this incomparable achievement.

The foundation stone was laid on the 22nd of May, 1720. The Residenz, 167 meters wide and 92 meters deep, has two side wings, each consisting of two closed blocks of construction with two inner courtyards. The two blocks are attached to the main cross lateral section in such a way as to create a Court of Honour of considerable depth. The Prince-Bishop entrusted the young architect Balthasar Neumann from Eger in Bohemia with the coordination of the building plans and justly so as the Würzburg Residenz is a unique and exuberant work of art. The building itself was completed on December 30, 1744, but its furnishing took decades to realize.

The Residenz, like so much of Würzburg, was almost totally burned out during the night of March 16, 1945. Due to an art lover, the American officer John D. Skilton, who had a protective roof installed, the original fresco paintings of Johann Zick and Giovanni Battista Tiepolo could be saved. Fresco painting, unlike secco painting, is done on wet plaster consisting of gypsum-free lime, sand, water and other leads. Upon drying, the surface forms a thin layer of calcium carbonate which is responsible for the longevity of the vivid colors and in the case of the Residenz, the reason that the ceiling paintings did not crack or flake off as they did in the Court Chapel.

The reconstruction of the Residenz has cost approximately 35 million marks to date. The Mirror Cabinet was first reopened in 1987.

Forty-two of the 342 rooms are furnished. In addition, the Martin-von-Wagner-Museum, university faculties, the Bavarian State Archives, the State Office for the Preservation of Historical Buildings, the Castle and Park Administration, private administrative apartments as well as – underground – the wine-pressing rooms and the decorative vat

Putti angels by Johann Peter Wagner.

cellars of the state run winery, the Hofkellerei (Court Cellars), are all housed within the Residenz's walls.

One of the most magnificent spatial creations ever achieved in architecture is Balthasar Neumann's Staircase above which is his even more superior unsupported vaulting. This ceiling was so ingeniously constructed that despite the serious doubts of the Viennese architect and Neumann rival, Lucas von Hildebrand, the over 600 square meter vault has held to this very day.

Prince-Bishop Carl Philipp von Greiffenclau employed Johann Zick, a south Geman, to paint the ceiling frescos "Diana in Repose" and "The Banquet of the Gods" in the Sala Terrena on the ground floor. But he left the decoration for Neumann's vault and the Imperial Hall (Kaisersaal) up to the imagination of the most eminent fresco painter of the period, Giovanni Battista Tiepolo. This single painting is the largest ceiling fresco in the world: a firmament of the gods above the four continents (at the time Australia was not yet included). Each continent is personified by a woman: "Europa" with a bull, "Asia" on an (African) elephant, "America" rides a giant alligator while "Africa" is enthroned on the back of a camel. A genuine global theater as Tiepolo imagined it covers the entire ceiling with liveliness and life. In the center, the sun rises and Apollo decends from the temple, his steeds held in waiting for him. Planets form a brilliant cluster around the prince-bishop magnifying his glory.

A total of 13 months was necessary to complete the ceiling fresco that Tiepolo with the assistance of his two sons, Domenico and Lorenzo, was only able to work on during the warmer months of the year aided by a free-standing scaffold. During the winter

Previous pages:
Residenz Staircase with Tiepolo frescos.
Right: The Residenz from the gardens.
Left: Details of Tiepolo's ceiling fresco.
Following pages: A concert in the Imperial Hall of the Residenz.

Mirror Cabinet (Spiegelkabinett).

work was carried out on the paintings for the side altars in the Court Chapel. Tiepolo and his assistants stayed "three years at court" and cost the prince-bishop the equivalent of around 1.5 million marks. This sum seems well-invested if one considers that nearly a half million visitors come to see the Residenz each year.

Among other things, the Imperial Hall offers an excellent view of the Court Gardens with Johann Peter Wagner's putti angels lending it an air of festivity. The entire garden as well as the Imperial Hall provide the ideal setting for the internationally famous Mozart Festival held each year in June. Famous orchestras, conductors and soloists have been performing here since 1922. Moreover, each year the Franconian Viticulture Association sponsors an exquisite Baroque Festival that also takes place in the Kaisersaal and within the walls of the fortress Marienberg.

The Imperial Hall was painted before the staircase ceiling and its decoration was not left up to Tiepolo's imagination but rather to a plan that had been laid down in writing and included specific historical events from Würzburg's past: the marriage of the Emperor Frederick Barbarossa to Beatrice of Burgundy (1156) and the investiture of Bishop Herold of Würzburg with the Duchy of Franconia by Barbarossa at the Reichstag in Würzburg (1168).

The ceiling painting depicts the allegory of the Genius Imperii. The sun god Apollo in his sun chariot drawn by four horses is bringing the young bride Beatrice to Barbarossa, the Genius Imperii.

The Imperial Apartments to the north and south of the Kaisersaal can be viewed with a guide and should not be missed. The Mirror Cabinet (Spiegelkabinett) is an absolute must. In addition, the Munich State Gallery has a permanent exhibit at the north end of the Residenz and the so-called Ingelheimer/Seinsheimer Room is furnished in the French decorative style that was combined with the new Classical style of the period.

The Hofkirche (Court Chapel) is located in the southwest corner of the Residenz. To be sure, a part of the chapel's brilliance is due to Balthasar Neumann's architectural concept of fitting Rococo oval vaults, lunettes and galleries into a rectangular outer shell. The history of the chapel's planning is both long and marked by vicissitudes. It was no simple matter for Neumann to defend his plans when famous architects like Boffrand, von Welsch, von Hildebrand or de Cotte had other ideas. Prince-Bishop Friedrich Carl von Schönborn, a man with plans of his own, was almost as difficult to convince. Yet Neumann did manage to sway the Prince-Bishop and the result is one of the most perfect religious edifices of the 18th century.

The Viennese, Lucas von Hildebrand, was commissioned to carry out the chapel's interior decoration – almost a simple matter in comparison to Neumann's task of inserting five oval vaults into the rectangular ceiling. The highly complex structure was further complicated by the fact that natural light could only enter through the south wall. Neumann's solution was ingenious. He made the south wall diagonal to allow more light to enter in through the windows. The vault was completed in 1733, the following year the interior decoration was decided upon including the second "double" altar above the High Altar for the Prince-Bishop's daily celebration of Mass. The design of the decoration is typical of the heavy Viennese Baroque. The completion of the Hofkirche was celebrated at its consecration on September 15, 1743.

Karl Körner of Munich renovated Johann Rudolf Byss's "secco" ceiling paintings which did not survive the Second World War. The Court Chapel's stucco decoration

The Sala Terrena in the Residenz with a ceiling fresco by Johannes Zick (1750); Following pages: Autumn in the Court Gardens.

and stucco figures are by Antonio Bossi while the statues on the altars are by Johann Wolfgang van der Auwera. The fine carving is the work of Adam Guthmann and the prie-dieus are by Ferdinand Hundt. The paintings on the side altars "The Fall of the Angels" and "The Assumption" are by Giovanni Battista Tiepolo. Confessionals were certainly uncalled for in the total design of the interior but two galleries were incorporated into the front and back of the chapel. The pillars are of Carrara marble and marble from Koblenz.

Layout plans for the Residenz Gardens were in the making from the very beginning of actual construction. Alterations in layout and design usually corresponded to the wishes of the ruling prince-bishop. At times the financial situation determined the extent that the plans could be carried out.

Adam Friedrich von Seinsheim who served as prince bishop from 1755-1779 was re-

sponsible for the layout of the palace gardens as we know them today. He wanted the bastions left as they were to dominate the terraced east gardens which were later expanded southwards. The electoral Bavarian Court architect, François Cuvilliers the Elder and Neumann's son, Franz Ignaz Michael as well as Johann Prokop Mayer from a town outside of Prague were all entrusted with the landscaping and care of the gardens. The superb palace garden gates are the work of the Tyrolean wrought-iron craftsman, Johann Georg Oegg, and the garden statues are by Johann Peter Wagner. Statues like "The Rape of Europa" and "The Rape of Proserpine" within the rondel at the south end of the gardens as well as the jovial putti angels in the arbors are not only delightful additions to the setting in the summertime when the roses are in full bloom and the Mozart Festival is in full swing, but even more so in the winter when the playful putti figures are mantled in white.

The Martin-von-Wagner Museum with its fine collection of Graeco-Roman art and print collection is also located in the south wing of the Residenz. Martin von Wagner (1777–1858) was a painter, sculptor and art collector as well as an art consultant and friend to the Bavarian king, Ludwig I.

Left: Court Chapel (Hofkirche) in the southwest corner of the Residenz.
Above: Balthasar Neumann.
Right: Greek vase on display in the university's Martin-von-Wagner Museum in the south wing of the Residenz.

Four Bottles of "Stein" Wine ...

... was Goethe's Christmas wish in 1808 and it just might have been that his supply of Franconian wines diminished considerably during the Christmas season. He had written to his wife in 1806: "Send me a few bottles of wine from Würzburg as no other wines taste good in comparison...". Whether or not he meant solely "Stein" wine, one of the oldest wines here that derives its name from its location, or whether he, like so many others, merely meant Franconian wine cannot be determined. As early as the 16th century the saying "the best wine grows on the Stein" was an indication of its quality. Franconian wines grow on various types of soil throughout the Main River Triangle and in the Steiger Forest: lime, muschelkalk, variegated sandstone, bedrock, clay, loess and keuper are some of the more common types of soil that in combi-

nation with the climate have such a distinct effect on the taste of the wines grown in this region. Franconian wines also contain a certain mineral content which is one of the reasons it is known as "wine for the sick".

The three large wineries – the Juliusspital, Bürgerspital and the Hofkellerei – each use

Above: Wine-tasting at the Old Crane with the Marienberg in the background.
Left: Red wine cellar of the state-run Court Cellars (Hofkeellerei) beneath the Residenz.
Right: A vintner carefully tests his wines in the Juliusspital.

Courtyard of the wine-inn "Zum Stachel".

one third of the Würzburg Stein vineyards. A 4.5 km nature trail winds up and around the "Stein". Naturally the "Stein" vineyards make up only a small portion of Franconia's 5000 hectares – wine grows as far north as Aschaffenburg and as far west as Hassfurt. During the Middle Ages the wine-growing area was ten times as large. Of the eleven wine-growing regions in Germany, Franconia ranks sixth in size.

For over 1200 years wine has been growing in Franconia – 150 to 400 meters above sea level. The first Franconian wine was officially mentioned in 777 in Hammelburg, in 779 in Würzburg. Today seven wine cooperatives, a few large wineries and numerous small vintners earn their living from entire hillsides covered with vines or from small individual patches of land given over to viticulture. Pfaffenberg, Schloßberg, Innere Leiste, Abtsleite and Kirchberg are a few of the well-known wine-growing regions.

A dozen or so small, picturesque wine villages have grown up along the bends of the Main River. In 1665 the monk, Albrecht Degen from the Cisterician abbey in Ebrach, introduced the traditional Silvaner variety to Franconia. Although the grape variety Müller-Thurgau has since replaced it in popularity, the genuine Franconian still swears by his Silvaner. A rich variety of grapes – Riesling, Bacchus, Rieslaner, Kerner, Scheurebe, Traminer plus a few red wine varieties – ensures a wide assortment of quality wines. The characteristic "Bocksbeutel" was created by the Bürgerspital in 1718 in order to further document the quality of wine grown on these hills. The bottle gets its name from its distinctive shape and refers to the testes of a goat or the shape of a Franconian peasant's bottle. Franconian wines can be enjoyed in the atmospheric wine-cellars of Würzburg, at one of the innumerable street wine festivals held in the neighboring villages throughout the summer months or simply in one of the many authentic wine inns that also serve hearty Franconian fare. Everything from the dry quality wines to the wines made only from the ripest grapes can be savored.

In 1990 the "House of Franconian Wines" near the Old Crane opened its doors and offers a unique opportunity to become acquainted with a "Schoppen" (1/4 litre) of fine Franconian wine in a pleasant atmosphere.

Above: Franconian still life. Below: Wine festival in the courtyard of the Bürgerspital.
Following Pages: Picking grapes on the slope above St. Burkard's.

Oberzell Convent on the Main River.

The Environs of Würzburg

The Main River meanders through the idyllic Franconian countryside in and around Würzburg. One wine village follows another, each with its surrounding hills and val-

leys covered in vineyards whose names are well-known to wine-lovers. Tucked away in many of these villages are lesser known treasures and sights waiting to be discovered: medieval Town Halls, Market Places with pinnacled gables and half-timbered buildings, town fortifications complete with towers and ring walls with narrow gates, churches and chapels, castles with and without moats, wells and gushing fountains in gardens and parks, and old monastic buildings.

One of these is the Convent Oberzell whose towers stand out proudly against the backdrop of autumn on the left side of the Main River just outside the city limits. Balthasar Neumann redesigned the former 12th century Premonstratensian abbey between 1744 and 1766. The convent with its lovely Baroque staircase is still used today by a religious order.

Left: Baroque staircase in the Convent Oberzell.

St. Vitus and the Rococo

He is one of the guardian saints and his remains lie at rest in St. Veit's Cathedral in Prague. He is seated as the beloved symbol of the town in a three-legged yellow pot on a red shield and has been the patron saint of Veitshöchheim since 1563. St. Veit, Latin: Vitus; "Höchheim" – literally high home or settlement on the hill. Towns with "Höchheim" in their names indicate settlements that date back to the middle of the 6th century. Archeological findings reveal settlements in the area that date back to the Neolithic and the Bronze Ages.

In addition to the Baroque church St. Veit's and a Romanesque tower from the 13th century, this picturesque town also has a lovely chapel (Martinskapelle) from the 12th century.

The Bavarian Landesanstalt for Viticulture and Horticulture is a member of the community just as much as the Main River Commerical Shipping Company, a chamber opera, and numerous restaurants, wine inns and private wineries that serve their own wine and sandwiches.

It is most likely that Veitshöchheim's advantageous location swayed the prince-bishops into purchasing land here in 1619 and to having a combination summer and hunting palace built (1680-1682) in this charming setting.

Balthasar Neumann redesigned the summer residence in 1752. Eleven years later, Prince-Bishop Adam Friedrich von Seinsheim commissioned the landscaping of the renowned Rococo Garden which is delightfully adorned with the statues and putti figures by such famous sculptors as Ferdinand Tietz, Johann Peter Wagner and Johann Wolfgang van der Auwera.

Summer palace in Veitshöchheim.

The park, which is 500 meters long and 270 meters wide, is divided into two parallel sections crossed by two main walkways. The entire park is an elaborate and labyrinth-like network of narrow paths and rows of high hedges that convey the feeling of being in a maze – a perfect place for a game of hide-and-seek. It is also the ideal setting for a moment of contemplation, either on a park bench in one of the many garden pavilions or around the large pond where Apollo and the Muses are reclining on Parnassus while Pegasus rears at the top. A smaller pond as well as manifold fountains, cascades, temples and grottos like the "Schneckenhaus" (Snail House) by Materno Bossi (1772/73) provide for amusement and relaxation. The palace underwent a total renovation between 1971 and 1981 during which time copies of 244 of the park's around 330 statues were made to replace the originals throughout the gardens.

Allegory of Spring by Ferdinand Tietz, around 1765.

Pavilion in Rococo Garden in Veitshöchheim.